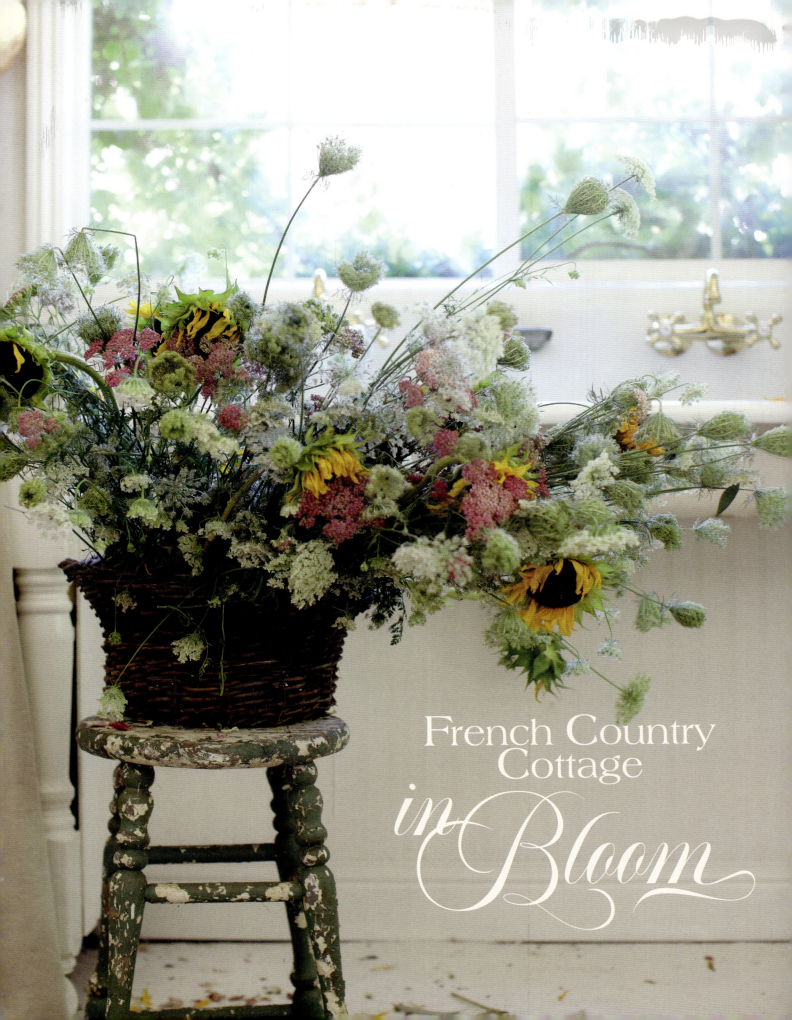

French Country Cottage
in Bloom

French Country Cottage
in Bloom

Courtney Allison

Gibbs Smith

To my husband and garden-loving family who have all inspired me to indulge in my love of flowers and to create a home filled with blooming beauty.

Contents

Living with Flowers 9

Flowers At Home 13

Arrangements for Entertaining 47

Cottage Garden Inspirations 73

Celebrate with Flowers 101

Inspired Florals Every Day 131

Touches of Whimsy 145

Creating Arrangements 175

Sourcing Flowers 220

A Few Thoughts on
Living with Flowers

Since childhood I have been enamored with beautiful blooms, from the pepper-scent garden roses behind my home to the dainty flowers on my favorite flannel nightgown. Flowers and a floral-filled way of living has always been part of my world.

As a child, I would stop and smell the roses, literally. I admired the smallest of delicate flowers growing between stacked rocks as well as the roses larger than my hand that grew in the garden. In California, the abundance of different flowers and places they grew always inspired me. I grew up where there were old orchards full of fruit trees and walnut groves, with houses tucked in among them. Our house had citrus trees on one side, and the scent from those pretty white blossoms would float in through the windows and fill the room with sweetness.

Each season offered an abundance of beautiful blooms and natural scenes. The open spaces of rolling hills were covered with poppies and wildflowers every spring and with tall, golden grasses in summer. Autumn brought a landscape covered in oak leaves, acorns, and rosy, warm rose hips. Even in winter, when the hillsides and trees were bare, there was beauty in the frost settling on the grasses and ground.

I spent much of my childhood out in nature. I remember getting lost in my playhouse for hours, with flowered curtains covering windows and a small table that was perfect for a tiny jar filled with a handful of flowers. It felt like a fairy-tale cottage in bloom. As I grew, my obsession continued with my Laura Ashley flannel nightgown that had lovely little yellow flowers. At the craft store, I chose ditsy fabrics with small, scattered flowers. The frilly, lace-covered bedding on my canopy had delicate embroidered flowers.

As an adult, I have been drawn to the romantic feeling that flowers bring to different rooms. I nearly always have a bouquet of flowers in the house—and a small pitcher of blooms in the bathroom or on a windowsill to bring a little burst of happy. I love floral fabrics and patterns, floral-painted furniture, and carved flowers on some of our antique furniture and mirrors. When it comes to arrangements of flowers in our home, I am not fussy. While I love to create a fancy arrangement just like everyone else, I often choose just a handful of fresh-cut garden roses or peonies in a simple vintage bucket—and I tend to enjoy those blooms a bit longer than they are fresh. When they get a tad wilted and drop petals, it is almost like a second bloom to me. The beauty of the blooms in the garden, in the vase, and in a beautiful disarray as they drop petals speaks romance to me and fuels my creativity.

When my husband and I moved into our house, we started to plant things in the yard to create a home with gardens and flowers all around. We were young and were renovating as we could and on a modest budget, so any big-scale plans were put on hold. So, what I brought home to plant were the three for $10 gallon specials from the grocery store. That is where I found my first foxglove and instantly fell in love with its old-fashioned English garden look.

Though our home was far from looking like a country cottage with a European-inspired garden, I planted a dozen foxgloves and enjoyed them. Each year, we would add a few plants, not having a master plan. I brought home whatever pretty faces I found and plopped them into the garden. I mostly stayed true to my favorite colors and greenery, and bit by bit, the garden areas started to come together. After several years, a lovely, rambling, layered look started to take shape.

We now have a dedicated cutting garden where we have planted many of my favorites: peonies, garden roses, and foxgloves are on repeat and mingle with many herbs and other beautiful flowers. Though I struggle with clipping too many blooms at a time, I do love seeing them in the garden as much as in the house. I am much inspired by the rambling English cottage garden look.

As we worked to restore the outside of our 1940s cottage, the dark old wood was replaced with fresh white cottage siding, and each window was dressed with a window box that my dad made from a fallen redwood fence. Every spring they become windows "in bloom," welcoming guests as they arrive and giving me a charming garden feeling while looking out.

Over the years, my style has evolved as much as the garden has grown and changed too. But one thing that has remained consistent in my aesthetic is my love of all those beautiful florals that I first discovered as a child—from collected china, tabletop items, architectural elements, and furniture with floral decoration to fabrics, tickings, flower-filled dresses, and, of course, fresh flowers in abundance.

My flower philosophy is simple: Flowers make me happy. So, I indulge in them and believe a fresh bouquet belongs in every room—even if it is just a tiny one.

You may have already discovered the varieties of flowers that speak to you. I encourage you to plant them in your garden or greenhouse and enjoy them as they bloom. Clip a few to take inside so you can soak up their scent and add beauty, or leave them in the garden to enjoy as you wander through and tend to the blooms— or both. A flower-filled lifestyle is a beautiful one.

This book is full of whimsical settings, simple arrangements to make and enjoy, vignettes in the house and garden, ideas for entertaining, and inspiration for seeking beauty in blooms. I hope that something in these pages speaks to you and inspires you to create flower-filled magic in your own home.

The method to my "flowers in the house" madness? I subscribe to the more-is-more philosophy and indulge it everywhere in our home, whether that is several pitchers or jars filled with fresh-cut blooms, a big, old copper pot or wooden bucket full of flowers on the dining room table, or smaller flower moments on the nightstand or in the bathroom. Flowers sprinkled throughout the house add a burst of sunshine and bring immeasurable warmth and charm as I meander from room to room.

Just like you would add a painting, a rug, seasonal knickknacks, or other decorative accents to a room when decorating, think of pretty flowers as part of your decor as well. That can be something as simple as a small bottle holding a single bloom in the bathroom or as big as a plentiful arrangement on the kitchen island.

In my opinion, flowers don't have to be perfectly designed, perfectly fresh, or even arranged in perfectly "proper" vessels to bring beauty. I always say, go with what makes you happy and makes you smile with any kind of decor. For a whimsical touch, consider using a unique vessel filled with a symphony of blooms for unexpected radiance in places you would not expect to find fresh flowers—like a bouquet placed on a chair in the hallway or tucked into an open cupboard. A floral-filled garland or simple crown draped on a mirror is a lovely display for dried blooms. A mishmash of several favorites arranged together, or even the simplest arrangement with just a single beautiful flower, can bring warmth and cheer to your home.

LEFT: Fresh-cut lilacs fill the kitchen with an intoxicating scent.
OVERLEAF: Vases of flowers along the counter wait to be mingled and arranged into different bouquets.

OPPOSITE AND ABOVE: Garden roses are favorites because of their ruffles and intoxicating scents. Here they are mixed with peonies and Queen Anne's lace in a traditional arrangement.
OVERLEAF: The most beautiful coral peonies start out vibrant and fade to a soft peach color. Filling an antique wooden trough creates a beautiful dining room vignette. **PAGE 22:** Soft, pale blooms in an old tobacco tin brighten a cupboard. **PAGE 23:** Butterfly ranunculus add a wispy touch to grocery store flowers.

OPPOSITE: Anemones in vintage silver add to a gilded vignette. **THIS PAGE, CLOCKWISE FROM TOP LEFT:** Foxgloves in an old wooden bucket create a sweet cottage garden moment. Peonies inside the potting shed waiting to be arranged is charming by itself. A pop of pretty, bold anemones and ranunculus on a bike by the camellia tree. Vintage glass seltzer bottles and pale blue hydrangeas are a perfect match. Peonies on a chair in the bathroom add a whimsical moment by the bathtub. Sometimes a simple, single flower arrangement is perfect—like sweet peas on a windowsill. Garden roses and ranunculus are arranged in a small pitcher. Vintage blue bottles filled with stock are a bit of whimsy on the potting shed windowsill.

ABOVE: In the attic, floral wallpaper and hand-painted floral beds mingle with a seasonal bouquet on an old trunk, which adds another layer of loveliness. **OPPOSITE:** Garden roses and spray roses with waxflowers in a vintage floral pitcher are a lovely touch on an old stool by the vintage floral ticking fabric-covered daybed.

FLOWERS AT HOME

OPPOSITE AND ABOVE: A bouquet of pastel dahlias and garden roses in a vintage silver pitcher on the nightstand is a sweet touch of sunshine. Hand-painted florals on the antique mirror add another layer of blooming beauty.

Peonies on the kitchen island are ready to be clipped and arranged into beautiful bouquets. Peonies are some of my favorite flowers, and when it is peony season, it is such a treat to enjoy bunches and bunches of them in the house. I enjoy arrangements full of mixed or single varieties of flowers, like peonies, ranunculus, garden roses, lilacs, and so many others for their beauty. And when flowers also have a delicious scent, it is even more lovely to have them scattered around the house.

OPPOSITE AND ABOVE: A selection of moody blooms is perfect for this mantel setting, while the white vintage tureen sets them apart from the background.

Peonies and garden roses are some of my favorite bouquets, by themselves or woven together. **OPPOSITE:** Several colors of peonies and garden roses fill the vase, and lisianthuses provide a little bit of drape effect. **ABOVE LEFT:** Pink peonies star in the chair bouquet, and white peonies, roses, and purple foxglove are combined in the arrangement on the floor. **ABOVE RIGHT:** This vintage garden pot was given to me by my grandfather when we moved into our home. Using pieces with special meaning give bouquets more import.

OPPOSITE: A garden gathering of foxgloves, garden roses, sweet peas, and peonies created a most lovely tall bouquet in the cottage kitchen. ABOVE: A basketful of fresh-clipped flowers waiting to be arranged is a beautiful blooming moment.

ABOVE AND OPPOSITE: I believe that flowers belong in every room of the house; the bathroom is no exception.

OPPOSITE: Flowers soaking in a farmhouse sink are always a beautiful view. **ABOVE:** Some of my favorite flowers are full of pale pastel and apricot hues, like these dahlias and Juliet roses.

Arrangements for Entertaining

I think I could set a table with gorgeous flowers every day of the week and not tire of playing with different looks and layers of loveliness. Table settings are all about layers, and the first layers I think of when planning a gathering are elegant flowers. From a garland with fresh flowers tucked in that creates a meandering, low centerpiece to bouquets of blooms dancing down the table to flowers in the background for even more ambiance—each has its place at the table.

I am most interested in how each layer tells a part of the table's story. From big buckets or gathered-up decanters or bottles to garlands draped down the center of the table and desserts topped with food-safe flowers, a table enhanced with gorgeous, interesting flowers is all about sharing my love of floral-filled everything with my guests.

Some of my favorite tables have one-flower arrangements. You can go bold and beautiful by repeating a single flower in a vase or by amassing a showy arrangement of one variety and color of blooms. Lilacs, larkspur, and delphinium are some of my favorites for designing tall arrangements that have more height than width, but sometimes I make them large all around for a whole lot of drama. For smaller arrangements that repeat down the table, I love ruffly blooms like garden roses, peonies, and ranunculus. Of course, a mix of both creates a lovely custom design. And just like in designing your home, there is no right or wrong way for your flowers to be arranged. If they make you smile when you look at them, they are just right.

Whatever way you decide to set your table with flowers, the beauty and the scent of fresh flowers and greens makes a table all the more enchanting.

Lilacs and lilac-colored roses in vintage blue-and-white porcelain is a classic look.

ARRANGEMENTS FOR ENTERTAINING

ABOVE AND OPPOSITE: Blue and purple larkspur in old jars with vintage linens on a chippy farm table create a touch of nostalgia for this breakfast room. **OVERLEAF:** Collected vintage plates and linens and a soft glow from the candles creates an unfussy setting.

OPPOSITE AND ABOVE: Arrangements of lilacs and roses paired with blue-and-white linens is classically elegant for a spring garden party.

ABOVE: Juliet roses are some of my favorites year-round. They don't need any companion flowers to create a stunning centerpiece. OPPOSITE: For a special occasion, we set an antique fountain piece on a round table and filled it with flowers. We also tucked greens and flowers into the chandelier. Together, the plentiful blooms and sizable antique statuary made a dramatic impression.

ARRANGEMENTS FOR ENTERTAINING

Dahlias are some of my favorite flowers to use in big arrangements and little ones. **ABOVE**: Dahlias are also lovely for decorating a cake. Here, three large heads on top of the cake rest on a thin barrier of waxed or parchment. **OPPOSITE**: Just a few stems slipped into collected thrift store bottles amass into a gorgeous centerpiece.

OPPOSITE AND ABOVE: A bucketful of purple and white larkspur is all that is needed for a stunning outdoor table. When setting the table outdoors, sometimes an abundance of a single flower variety gathered in a bucket can make the biggest impression.

A table set next to a blooming arbor creates an idyllic backdrop for an outdoor gathering. One of my favorite things about planning a gathering is wandering around the yard, looking for the perfect backdrop for the table. Our front garden arbor is covered with Cecile Brunner roses every spring, and their soft, barely blushing white flowers are gorgeous. As their petals fall, they create a lovely carpet of blooms underfoot. I was inspired to set a small table next to the arbor and gather up all their magic by candlelight.

While I often prefer to leave the table's patina uncovered, I also like a tablecloth that adds a bit of personality. This buffalo-check flax linen brings a warm, French country layer to the setting. The soft sage color is repeated on the vintage dishes and mixes beautifully with the chunky vintage goblets and pine-green swirl candles.

The centerpiece is an abundance of white garden roses and ruffled peonies set in a vintage tureen. A tip about arrangements in shallow vessels is to use a flower frog and also tape across the top to help keep flowers in place. I use big, full blooms and clip them shorter so they fill the container and spill over the edges just a bit.

OPPOSITE AND ABOVE: For this table under the oak tree, garlands on the table and overhead display an abundance of floral ambiance. Arrangements are placed on the wine barrels in the background, and the candles were tucked into bottles and decanters for a whimsical touch.

OPPOSITE AND ABOVE: Juliet roses with a pop of blue larkspur in a bucket make a sweet country-style arrangement for the table. **OVERLEAF:** Cottage garden roses and a few sprigs of thyme are lovely in an old wicker basket.

Cottage Garden
Inspirations

Every time I tend to my garden I think of my grandfather. When we first bought our home, he came by and looked at all of the overgrown plants and shrubs we had on our acreage and told me what each one was and how to tend to it. While Gramps was a neat and tidy type of gardener, I am more the kind that likes rambling, overgrown, and somewhat unruly. I love to crowd more plants into the beds and fill them up with layers.

One of the first things we planted in the garden and bed areas around the house was roses. In abundance. And everywhere. The first climbing rose I brought home to this house was Cecile Brunner. I found several five-gallon pots of them at the garden center but had no idea what they would look like or grow like; I just went by the little tag attached with a photo of the flowers in bloom, and they looked lovely. They took off the first year we planted them and have grown a huge amount since then, enough that they toppled the archway they were trained on. We did our best to salvage it and rebuild in place, then we pushed the roses back onto the arbor. Now, a literal wall of roses grows on one side of the arch each spring from the canes that fell a bit—an unexpected but delightful twist in what could have been a big pile of dead branches.

Some of the best climbers in cottage gardens are Eden roses. You simply can't beat their cabbage rose shape and long-lasting flowers. Some of my garden and climbing favorites are Earth Angel, Pretty in Pink Eden, Ingenious Mr. Fairchild, New Dawn, Colette, Le Petite Prince, and Quicksilver.

The potting shed garden filled with foxgloves, lambs ear, and peonies is bathed in the golden glow of sunset light.

OPPOSITE: An antique harvest bucket makes a beautiful vessel for big, bushy blooms like these lilacs. ABOVE: Rows of purples and blues looks just as pretty growing tall in the garden beds as they do in cut arrangements.

ABOVE AND OPPOSITE: Old-fashioned garden roses and ranunculus in the sweetest shades of pink pair beautifully with vintage furniture and the camellia tree.

ABOVE: A favorite vintage cart filled with flowers in the garden is a charming picture. **OPPOSITE:** A close-up of the vintage cherub fountain in the rose garden. **OVERLEAF:** I love this old wooden market cart in the garden even more when it is filled with fresh-clipped flowers. It is also a perfect cart to bring along while deadheading plants.

ABOVE: The lion fountain has a lovely carpet of ivy and Cecile Brunner roses that have grown over from the back side. **OPPOSITE, CLOCKWISE FROM TOP LEFT:** Wisteria blooms, Cecile Brunner archway; cherry blossoms in the afternoon sun; lilacs in a wooden cart.

OPPOSITE AND ABOVE: The garden cart is filled with foxgloves just ready to be planted in the beds. Foxgloves are one of my favorite garden flowers. We have many of them on both sides of the potting shed path. *Note:* Foxgloves are poisonous, so be mindful about planting them if you have pets or children that go into your garden areas.

ABOVE LEFT: A pot full of happy anemones. **ABOVE RIGHT AND OPPOSITE:** Fresh-clipped peonies in baskets and buckets along with foxgloves and lilacs say "spring" in the greenhouse.

OPPOSITE: In early spring, the wisteria begins to fill the front of the greenhouse with blooms. When those flowers are gone, Eden climbing roses fill in the greenery. ABOVE: Inside the potting shed is where I play with potted and clipped flowers. OVERLEAF: Baskets of peonies have been gathered from the garden.

ABOVE: A garden table sits by the flower beds behind the greenhouse. OVERLEAF: In spring, foxgloves create a beautiful pathway as they bloom copiously amid roses, lilacs, and peonies.

A few garden moments, CLOCKWISE FROM TOP LEFT: Potted lavender. Our chickens follow us wherever we go in the yard; the rose garden is their favorite spot to scratch while we do garden work. Still life of secateurs and blooms on a stool. Kevin the goat climbs on a chair amid the wild sweet peas. A foggy look at the greenhouse with Eden roses in bloom. A close-up of wisteria on the greenhouse. Under the blossoming apple tree, layers of foxglove grow tall.

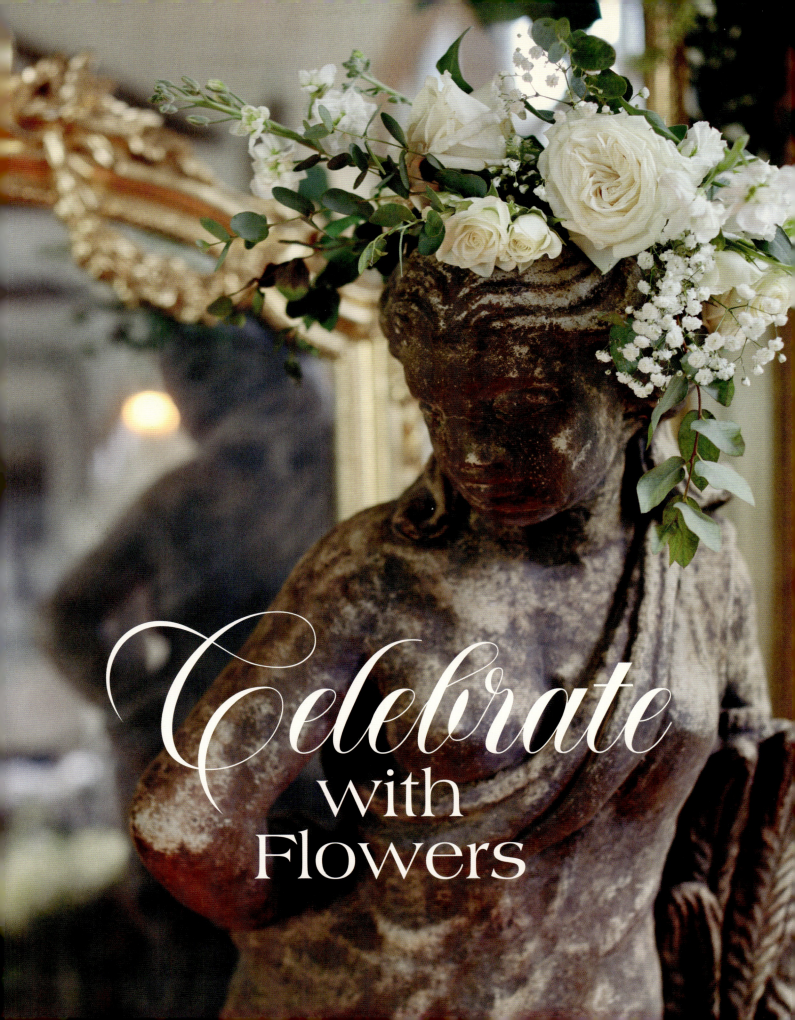

Celebrate
with Flowers

When one of my sons and his fiancé were planning a destination wedding, they asked me to create the flowers for the big family reception that would take place afterward. Playing with flowers is something I always enjoy, so, with a few notes from my future daughter-in-law about what she liked, I chose varieties for an abundance of flowy white arrangements and ordered custom baby's breath garlands for ten tables.

It was the first time I had been involved with planning a very large order of flowers for a big event and needed to consider the timing for the delivery. The flowers would need to be ready for arranging and be blooming throughout the event (garden roses need time to open fully, and hydrangeas can be fickle, for example). The flowers were delivered on time and in good shape, and after arranging the individual arrangements and adding flowers to the baby's breath garlands, they all opened up right on time and lasted more than a week after the big reception.

More recently, I did the flower arrangements for my brother's large wedding and for my oldest son's vineyard wedding as well. Though I certainly admit my flower obsession, I didn't initially set out to do event florals; but it seems that creating wedding and special-occasion flowers has become a blooming part of my business—and I absolutely love it! Each event is different, with different visions and ideas for the ambiance; bringing a dream design to life for a special day for someone is a delight for me as well. I have learned a few tricks along the way, from working within a certain budget to designing custom florals for arches and sweetheart tables to creating an abundance of romantic ambiance wherever the event is located. With each event I work on, I learn something new and am inspired to create many more beautiful settings for celebrating beautiful moments.

For a lavish garden party, a vintage Ralph Lauren sheet makes a flowery tablecloth under the well-filled flower arrangements.

ABOVE AND OPPOSITE: Flower-topped cakes are some of my favorites. You can special order at your local bakery or create your own. *Note:* Always be sure to research that any real flowers used are food safe. Also use a barrier sheet of parchment or waxed paper, or use flower cake spikes to hold the flowers up so they do not directly touch the cake. Optionally, faux flowers or sugar flowers can provide the look you want.

OPPOSITE AND ABOVE: Juliet roses by themselves or paired with thyme have an air of simple luxury.

ABOVE AND OPPOSITE: A vintage baby buggy filled with a mix of spring flowers was a perfect container for the baby shower centerpiece for welcoming our first grandchild. Florist foam tucked inside the buggy kept the flowers hydrated for the occasion, but a container of water set inside would work as well.

ABOVE AND OPPOSITE: A small, special occasion dinner party in the garden calls for a few singular touches, like filling the fountain with flowers and making a floral arch entrance to the table. We used a faux garland for the base of the arch and added fresh greens and flowers in abundance.

OPPOSITE AND ABOVE: On and around the table, thrift store glass vessels filed with white hydrangeas, roses, and baby's breath radiate elegance.

OPPOSITE AND ABOVE: Wedding arrangements in holding before they were loaded into the car created abundant flower moments.

OVERLEAF: Something about pretty blooms sitting on lovely old chairs inspires me. I love to capture flower-filled moments in unusual settings. Here, an antique French settee is set with a couple of the wedding bouquets and the sweetheart table floral swag.

ABOVE AND OPPOSITE: Decorating trees and garlands with fresh flowers is a delicious luxury for a winter wedding or other special occasion. Water vials will keep the flowers fresh longer.

ABOVE: A bouquet of lilies and roses for a beautiful bride. OPPOSITE: On the barrel, a large statement arrangement of garden roses and larkspur with vintage glasses and a Capodimonte candle holder made a nostalgic pause.

CELEBRATE WITH FLOWERS

OPPOSITE AND ABOVE: A trio of mirrors got a refresh for the wedding with fresh flower–filled garlands and arrangements. The vintage statue dons a fresh flower crown for the occasion. **OVERLEAF:** Dainty corsages and boutonnieres wait on a vintage platter to be given out.

OPPOSITE AND ABOVE: A mossy table under the oak with flowers and candles on repeat exudes a French country feeling for a late autumn wedding. **OVERLEAF:** The walkway with vintage buckets of flowers leads to a fresh-flower garland arch overlooking a stunning mountain view.

Inspired Florals
Every Day

Living with flowers means enjoying a flower-filled way of living that indulges in floral patterns, not just fresh-clipped flowers.

Vintage china, linens, furniture, artwork, wallpapers, and such that have floral patterns are lovely expressions that don't involve fresh flowers.

For example, floral artwork can be wonderful by itself or arranged in a collection and displayed on a wall. A cupboard that has precious flowers painted on the doors brings a lovely touch without any clipping needed. Place settings of collected vintage floral plates bring a nostalgic, romantic look to the table. A bedroom wrapped in floral wallpaper and layered with bedding in bloom can be an abundant look, and using wallpaper inside a cupboard creates a sweet moment every time the doors are opened.

As much as I adore finished bouquets, I am also enamored with flowers in the process of being arranged. Various vessels on the counters and flowers plopped in the sink for a long soak of water are pleasant all by themselves.

When those week-old flowers begin to fade, I find a certain loveliness in their softness and squish as they wilt, and I enjoy them much longer than while they are in perfect bloom. I don't mind mingling dried or less-than-fresh flowers with fresh-clipped blooms—some flowers are quite beautiful as they dry. And of course, when they begin to drop, the explosion of dainty petals underneath creates a charming "mess" that I like to enjoy for a bit longer.

LEFT: Dainty vintage floral art and a small bouquet form an appealing vignette on a table. **OVERLEAF**: Sweet peas and roses in a tiny gold-etched pitcher pair perfectly with an antique floral-carved cupboard.

ABOVE AND OPPOSITE: Purple and white blooms tucked into a vintage flower pot decorated with floral garland creates a spring moment. **OVERLEAF:** A vintage ironstone tureen is a sweet vessel for a summer arrangement full of pink and white blooms.

OPPOSITE AND ABOVE: Florals on furniture, fabrics, and dishes are things I enjoy collecting.

ABOVE AND OPPOSITE: Layers of lovely blooms abound—in the tablecloth, the dishes, and the arrangement.

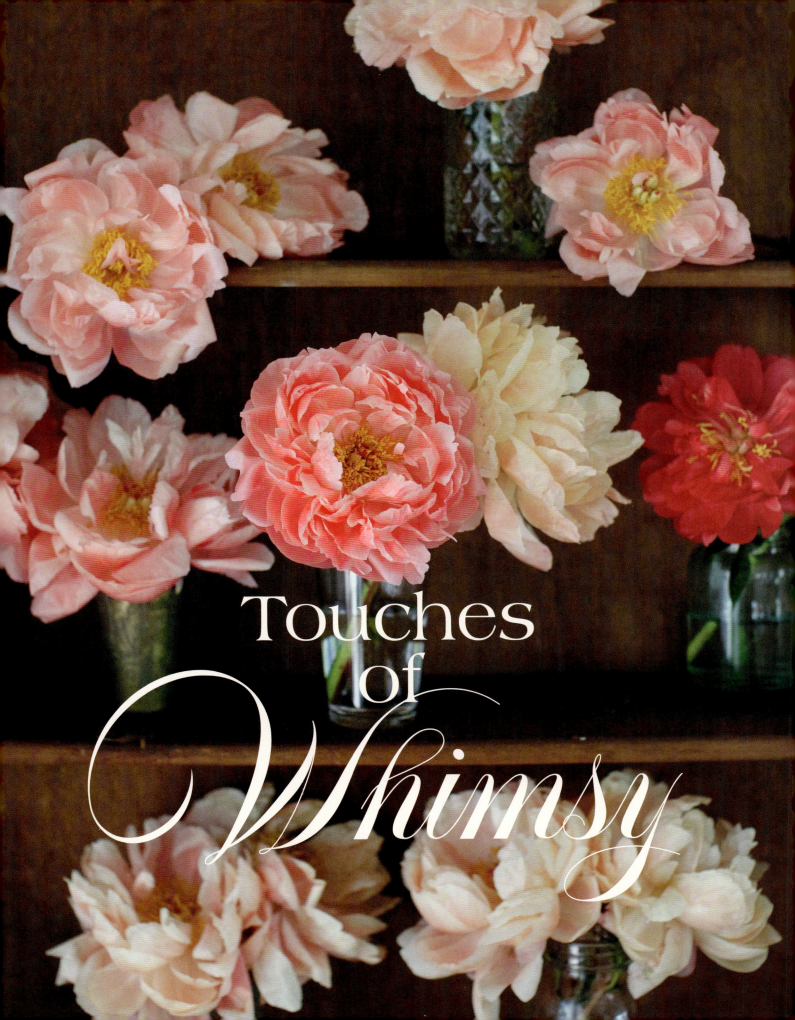

Touches of Whimsy

I am far from practical when it comes to a whimsical setting for a photo. I just go with what is speaking to me in the moment—such as an old settee covered in floral fabric with a bunch of farmers market flowers plopped on it.

Something about a bunch of fresh-cut flowers inspires my love of whimsy and photographing flowers in unexpected settings with out-of-the-ordinary props. My creative eye is drawn to unique elements that tell the story of a photo. For flower moments, these often involve vintage elements like chippy old painted boxes, interesting stools, and wooden chairs with a good patina. I scour flea markets, thrift shops, and online sources all year long for charming elements to use for styling. Various vessels, wooden crates, chippy tables, and weathered accessories talk to me and I take them home. And I cannot resist adding another vintage chair to my growing collection. For me, a beautiful old chair is perfect for taking photos of many things, like stacks of old linens, our sweet silkie chickens, beautiful cakes, floral arrangements, and other simple vignettes. For the perfect juxtaposition, a chair might be covered in luxe velvet, or it might be a simple wooden farmhouse chair with a delicate needlepoint, a gilded frame, or carved flowers adorning it. Even an old, deconstructed chair has beauty in its imperfections. Beautiful blooms and handsome vintage chairs go together perfectly.

Following my fanciful and whimsical side (as impractical as it might be at times) fuels my creative energy, and I love the magic that happens when that inspiration and whimsy come together and create a beautiful moment.

LEFT: I am always happy when playing with flowers and holding my chickens. My love of flowers shows on everything, including the charming, chintz-covered sofas. **OVERLEAF:** Our vintage Avion trailer is set up as an impromptu flower market stand for a special occasion. We stacked crates and filled buckets with flowers, creating a perfect backdrop for guest photos.

OPPOSITE AND ABOVE: Dahlias, wildflowers, roses, and more fill vintage wooden barrels and buckets.

OPPOSITE AND ABOVE: A vintage cot found at a tag sale is layered with flowered bedding and pillows, creating a charming spot for summertime reading. An old wooden bucket filled with flowers and grasses sits amid the wild-growing sweet peas underneath the old-growth cedar trees. Our silkie chickens love to wander and are always joining us while we are outdoors.

ABOVE AND OPPOSITE: A crystal-covered chandelier sets the stage for a flower-filled table under the oak tree. Vintage flower-covered pitchers serve as vases for fresh-clipped garden roses, larkspur, and seasonal flowers.

TOUCHES OF WHIMSY

OPPOSITE AND ABOVE: A vintage mauve chair in a field embraces a plop of colorful, romantic blooms.

OPPOSITE: A Chippendale-style sofa with floral ticking is a foil for a bundle of fresh flowers. **THIS PAGE:** Flower-filled everything makes me happy!

OPPOSITE: Peonies arranged in small jars on cupboard shelves create a whimsical look of aloha.
ABOVE: Peonies waiting in buckets are pretty enough to be lush bouquets. **OVERLEAF:** An antique settee covered in its original floral fabric is a delightful moment, especially with flowers plopped on the seat. **PAGES 166-67:** An antique wicker swing under the oak tree and fresh dahlias create a magic moment.

ABOVE AND OPPOSITE: A vintage decanter used as a candle holder and a plop of garden-gathered, dried, and grocery store flowers on a wine barrel table wait to be arranged for a whimsical setting.

ABOVE: A worn, well-loved deconstructed chair and a brass bowl floral arrangement create one of my favorite mingles of rustic and refined. OPPOSITE: Fresh dahlias and farmers market flowers in a vintage champagne bucket are perfection on a rosy antique chair.

ABOVE: After arranging several vases of flowers, I placed them in an open cupboard for display.
OPPOSITE: In an outdoor vignette, a French settee, a vintage trunk, and a white bouquet become a candlelit holiday moment.

Creating Arrangements

When creating bouquets, I don't have a tried-and-true-method for designing them or a recipe that I follow. I most often follow what is inspiring me in the moment. Whether you are stirred by a certain color, a variety, a mix of gathered flowers blooming in the garden, or dried flowers or faux, you can't go wrong if they make you happy.

I often clip fresh flowers, greens, and wildflowers from our yard to bring indoors. And I dry flowers all year long in the potting shed to incorporate in my floral decor. When I am heading to the flower market, my go-to list of greens is fairly consistent year-round: fresh eucalyptus in various shapes—like silver dollar, spiral, and gunni. It is a staple for arrangements, garlands, and simple swags. I also love fresh olive, which is lovely for floral arrangements and for garnishing tables or platters.

A few of my favorite flowers to bring home:

- Ranunculus—Cloni is delightful when available, as is the butterfly variety; but all the dainty ruffled varieties are beautiful.
- Lilacs—Pale lavender is my fav, but I haven't met a lilac I didn't love.
- Peonies—A shining star of cottage garden flowers, in my book.
- Garden roses—So many nostalgic varieties and colors to choose from, I have too many favorites to list. A bonus of those old-fashioned blooms is that many have an incredible scent.
- Larkspur and Stock—Unsung flower heroes, in my opinion. Both are tall and stately with beautiful petals. Stock smells delightful as well.
- Sweet peas—We have an abundance that grow naturally in our yard, but they can be found at the flower markets as well.
- Hydrangeas—Simple whites, blues, pinks, and greens are usually available at grocery stores, but the antique colors, burgundy, purples, and big pee gee hydrangeas are what I seek at the flower market.
- Dahlias—Another of my favorites, Cafe au Lait are delightful pale pink to peach blooms. I also love shades of whites, pinks, purples, and any color of the pom-pom ball and dinner plate varieties.
- Herbs, Berries, Garden Foliage—Often overlooked for floral arrangements, fresh herbs like rosemary, mint, and lavender add lovely color and scent. Foraging for foliage like ivy, spirea, etc. and tucking in a few wild blackberries is always a lovely addition.

PEONIES ON REPEAT: Single-variety arrangements are some of my faves. Here it is pink peonies in a blue-and-white jar. A small metal frog top keeps them in place, and some taller stems balance the fullness with a little height.

CREATING ARRANGEMENTS

DAINTY & DELICATE: White and pink dahlias and white and burgundy cosmos in a low ironstone vessel is a simple arrangement that creates a happy moment wherever you place it.

CREATING ARRANGEMENTS

AUTUMN BEAUTY: Arrangements that are full of rich, moody colors and dried accents set the tone for autumn. This one came together with several bunches of seasonal farmers market flowers and dried flowers from the grocery store. The final touch is to ease in some dried grasses and flowers that drape for drama and movement.

POP OF PRETTY: Some of my favorite colors of dahlia along with seasonal grasses, celosia, lisianthus, cosmos, zinnias, and echinacea comprise this bouquet. Start with grasses along the edge of the urn to create a soft "outside," fill the inside with a mix of flowers, and then arrange the flowers until it feels as full as you would like. Slip a couple more grasses into the center for a feeling of height.

CREATING ARRANGEMENTS

DELIGHTFUL DAHLIAS: Dahlia varieties in shades of peachy pinks with a few pops of bold color and creamy whites steal the show in a rusty, weathered urn. The key to an arrangement like this one is to fill the container with an abundance of blooms and then tuck in some taller ones to add a little drama.

FARMERS MARKET PRETTY: Daisies, dahlias, bachelor buttons, zinnias, statice, and more in bold colors are set off perfectly by a silver container.

CREATING ARRANGEMENTS

CREATING A FLOWER CROWN: Creating a fresh or dried flower crown is a lovely touch for a statue. Simply use stiff wire to wrap around the head of your statue and secure it for the right size crown. Then use craft wire or hot glue to add your flowers to the wire. A ribbon tied in the back would add a nice touch.

GROCERY STORE BEAUTY: A chicken wire pillow holds these blooms in place. Just cut a section of chicken wire and fold it over so there are several layers of the wire and then place it in your container. Alternatively, use a premade frog.

SIMPLE ROMANTIC BLOOMS: Stocks, roses, and sweet peas come together in a rustic, country-style arrangement. The purple jar is a romantic touch.

SEASONAL ABUNDANCE: Bunches of flowers, like butterfly ranunculus, tulips, poms, mums, asters, veronica, and more, create a romantic moment. The key to this one is to just use what is in season. All these flowers were found at the grocery store.

PETITE GARDEN-GATHERED: Small arrangements in a copper mold, a teacup, or a jewelry box make unique gifts. The copper mold has peonies and garden roses. The others have mixes of what was blooming in the garden at that moment. Foxgloves, garden roses, hellebores, anemones, and lilacs make sweet arrangements.

ROMANTIC NOSTALGIA: A favorite way to gift flowers is to wrap them in brown paper. Simply lay your flowers on the paper and then fold the bottom and the sides over the stems. Tie with twine or ribbon. This is a carry-home look you might see at a Parisian flower market.

CREATING ARRANGEMENTS

ONE BOUQUET TWO WAYS: The flowers shown on the preceding page are styled as a ribboned bouquet. Here they have been arranged in a pottery pitcher for a table bouquet.

CREATING ARRANGEMENTS

SUMMER SUNSHINE: This feels like bold summer sunshine in an antique urn on a pedestal. Don't overlook your antique statuary for arrangements; simply add a vessel, a frog, and fill with water and your preferred blooms.

VINTAGE ROMANCE: This sweet floral moment is composed of burgundy hellebore, Juliet roses, lilacs, and sweet peas in a vintage brass punch bowl. I used a traditional frog for this one and started by creating a base with the hellebore before adding the roses and sweet peas and finishing with the lilacs.

WHIMSICAL BEAUTY: This mix is made up of several bunches of white grocery store flowers, like daisies and statice, and echinacea from the garden. Several types of fresh eucalyptus greens, succulents, and a couple of dried lotus pods tucked in create a serene arrangement.

CREATING ARRANGEMENTS

SUMMER SUNSET: This vintage concrete planter pot was perfect for a mingling of flowers gathered from the garden. I added long clippings of thyme for some height and left the sweet peas long so they could dangle just a bit for a little drama.

CREATING ARRANGEMENTS

BOLD & BEAUTIFUL BLUE & PEACH: Bold and beautiful blues paired with garden roses is a stunning over-the-top arrangement.

ROMANTIC HEIRLOOM GARDEN ROSES: I love garden roses wrapped in paper, mingled with peonies, or arranged with stock in a vase. **OPPOSITE:** Garden roses stuck into a florist block in a vintage basket create an old-fashioned centerpiece.

AUTUMN BLUSH: A vintage tureen is a perfect vessel for an arrangement with Juliet roses. I added a chicken wire frog and tucked the flowers and foliage inside. Placed into an open cupboard, it creates a lovely blooming moment that is echoed by a smaller sugar container arrangement above.

Sourcing Flowers

I am often asked where I find all the beautiful flowers for my floral designs. The truth is, they come from several different places, and my sources vary seasonally. While I grow flowers that can be clipped and brought indoors, below are my most-loved places to find everyday and special-occasion flowers as well.

Flower Markets

If you have never walked into a large flower market to shop, I highly encourage you to find one and do that. My favorite is the San Francisco Flower Mart.

The flower market is like a playground for those who love fresh flowers. The smell of the blooms and greens as you walk in is intoxicating. All the buckets, shelves, and tables filled with fresh-clipped stems in each vendor space is a visual delight that makes me almost giddy. I often go without a detailed plan for shopping—meaning, I like to see what inspires and speaks to me. I may come home with an armful of antique hydrangeas, a basketful of creamy Café au Lait dahlias, and larkspur. Or maybe it will be the garden roses I can't resist that trip. It can, in some ways, feel overwhelming to be inspired by so many different blooms, grasses, and greens at one time; there is a feeling to bring them all home. So, I have learned to slow my pace, take my time to consider which direction to go in with that day's shopping, and curate the look I am after. Maybe that day, lavenders and sage greens speak to me. Or maybe it will be a bowl of cream peonies paired with a lovely Juliet garden rose. My advice is to look, listen to what is talking to you, and go with what inspires you.

To know: Some flower markets are not open to the public. You need a resale or business license to shop. But they might have days when the public can shop. Check into it before planning a trip.

Farmers Markets

Always a wonderful place to get a unique variety of local blooms, farmers markets have some of the most charming gathered bundles. I also believe in supporting small businesses, and by shopping the farmers market, I can do that right in my own backyard. *Tips*: Shop early for the best bunches. And get to know the farmers who sell the flowers you like best. Often, you will be able to arrange to shop the farm or special-order flowers for pickup on a day they are not selling at the market.

When traveling, I will do a little searching to see if there are any local markets to shop. Finding flowers that are unique to different areas is always a treat.

Grocery Stores

An overlooked gem for flowers is your local grocery store. While they may not all have a good variety of special or specific types of flowers available, if you find one that does, it can be a wonderful source for weekly flowers. A few of my favorites are Trader Joe's, Whole Foods, and Debi Lilly at Safeway. Supermarkets often have big bunches of 12 to 18 roses reasonably priced and even get some of the ruffled garden rose varieties on occasion. They usually have a good mix of seasonal flowers and elements as well.

It is worth asking about special orders too; the florist may be able to source and order something special for you.

Small Floral Shops

Smaller floral shops can be a treasure trove for more unique flowers and ready-to-go arrangements. They are usually higher in price, but it may be worth it for finding the varieties you love most the year-round.

Online Floral Shops

I have ordered flowers to be shipped from the flower market when I needed something special. There are also online farm-fresh flower sources that will ship as well. My go-tos are the San Francisco Flower Mart, Petaldriven, and Grace Rose Farm. They often source from growers in your local area and will ship overnight. They can also ship special flowers like peonies off-season by shipping from other growers around the world.

Neighbors and Friends

Some of your neighbors might be more than willing to let you go over and trim flowers that are growing like weeds at their house. Not everyone enjoys gardening or loves overgrown, rambling, English-cottage garden style, and they would appreciate the trim and cleaning up that comes with clipping blooms.

Faux Flowers

Realistic faux flowers can be enjoyed by themselves or be blended with fresh ones to fill out an arrangement. My *French Country Cottage*-inspired French Market and Marseille Meadow collections are available at Balsam Hill.

Thank You

To my family for always believing in me and supporting all my crazy ideas and helping to make them happen. I love each of you so very much.

Special thanks to my husband for always keeping our home in bloom and bringing flowers home for me to play with all year long. To you and Ansley for carting flowers, moving furniture, tending the gardens, and setting up all the flower-filled moments as I worked on this book. I couldn't have done it without your help.

To my children, Ryan, Cullan and Ansley, and their loves, Katt, Diem and Harley, along with our sweet grandbabies, Juliette, Enzo, Jionni, Sophie and Jiovanni: you each bring so much joy to us and you inspire me every day to create beauty and whimsy for your world.

To my gramps for teaching me all about how to grow beautiful blooms and tend gardens. To my dad for teaching me how much magic landscaping and overfilled cottage window boxes add to a home. To my Mom, Scott, and siblings, Chris, Evan and Taylor, for your encouragement and support of me always.

To Jill Cohen for your help in bringing *In Bloom* to print and to Madge Baird for your support and patience as I worked on this book.

To my flower-loving *French Country Cottage* friends and community for taking time out of your day to read my ramblings, for your notes and kindness, and for your support of my books and blog. *French Country Cottage* would not be what it is without each of you.

The Author

Courtney Allison founded the lifestyle blog and brand *French Country Cottage*, a place inspired by renovations of her 1940s cottage and about living a lifestyle that is fueled by inspiration and the romance that comes with it. She loves the quintessential mix of rustic and elegant elements, indulges a love of all things sprinkled with ambiance and magic, and believes that a chandelier and bouquets of fresh flowers belong in every room.

In addition to working as an influencer, she is a freelance photographer, stylist, and floral designer. Her work has been featured in magazines and websites in the U.S. and Europe.

A mom of three grown children and grandmother of five, Courtney lives in a little slice of the countryside in California with her husband and their flock of silkie chickens and pair of mischievous goats. She loves to travel and discover new inspirations, taking camera in hand, playing with flowers, and creating moments of whimsy. Connect with Courtney and *French Country Cottage* on her blog, Facebook, and Instagram.

First Edition
29 28 27 26 25   5 4 3 2 1

Text © 2025 by Courtney Allison
Photographs © 2025 by Courtney Allison

All rights reserved. No part of this book may be reproduced by any means whatsoever without written permission from the publisher, except brief portions quoted for purpose of review. No part of this book may be used or reproduced in any manner for the purpose of training artificial intelligence technologies or systems.

Published by
Gibbs Smith
570 N. Sportsplex Dr.
Kaysville, Utah 84037
1.800.835.4993 orders
www.gibbs-smith.com

Designed by Rita Sowins / Sowins Design

Printed and bound in China
This product is made of FSC®-certified and other controlled material.

Library of Congress Control Number: 2023945638
ISBN: 978-1-4236-6259-4